MW01168978

Dary's Cookbook

Dary Medrano

NEWMAN SPRINGS PUBLISHING
320 Broad Street
Red Bank, NJ 07701

First originally published by Newman Springs Publishing 2024

ISBN 979-8-89308-250-0 (Hardcover)
ISBN 979-8-89308-249-4 (Digital)

Printed in the United States of America

About Me

Hello, my name is Dary Medrano. I am a Latina, raised in New York City and born in the Dominican Republic. I am a mother, wife, author, designer, and creator. Growing up, food was always the glue that brought my family together. Whether it was learning from my parents in the kitchen or sitting at the dining table sharing meals while talking about life.

Through my cookbook, I hope to bring that same sense of warmth, connection, and joy to your home that food has brought to mine. Welcome to my kitchen, let's create something delicious together!

Acknowledgment

Thank you to my husband and my kids for always believing in me. This one is dedicated to you. You gave me the strength and courage to believe in myself. I don't know where I would be without you.

Thank you to my mother, stepfather, and mother-in-law for teaching me and sharing your secrets of your kitchen with me which helped me be the amazing cook I am today.

Last but certainly not least, thank you, God, for always being by my side and guiding me into fulfilling my dreams.

Love,
Dary

Introduction

As a little girl, I remember standing by my stepfather's side, just staring at him as he would create these delicious meals with such ease and love. The aroma in the kitchen was amazing and something I would look forward to each day. No matter what I was doing, as soon I heard him in the kitchen, I would stop and immediately go stand next to him for the next hour, asking him all sorts of questions about what he was making. No matter how many questions I would ask, he was always happy to answer.

As I got older, he let me be more hands-on, which was so exciting. I truly mastered the art of cooking and made it into my own when I left my parents' house at seventeen years old. I had my first child and felt that I had to learn everything there was to learn to feed my daughter healthy and delicious meals she wouldn't be able to refuse. Of course, with the help of my mother just a phone call away and everything I had learned from my stepfather, cooking became a whole new world to me. Nowadays I cook for my family of six.

I love to cook and love creating meals my family loves. Hearing them tell me how delicious everything was and seeing the beautiful smiles on their face means the world to me.

I wrote this cookbook to share my top 10 favorite recipes you can share with your friends and family, ranging from Latin cuisine to Italian delicacies, along with my personal stories, and childhood memories. These recipes are a must-have at my home. I hope once you make it, you also feel the same warmth and love I feel every time I make it. Enjoy!

Dary's Beef Lasagna

I first fell in love with this meal when I first tried it at my aunt's house at the age of twelve. I would look forward to Sunday dinners with our entire family—cousins, aunts, and grandparents. This was always my request to my aunt whether we were having dinner at my house or hers. Today every time I eat it, it brings me back to that little girl I once was. Like everything I make, I always put my own twist to make it my own with flavors and ingredients that I love.

Ingredients: (serves 10)
- Baking lasagna pan
- 1 box lasagna
- 2lb 20/80 fat ground beef
- 1lb shredded mozzarella cheese
- 1 small ricotta
- 1 medium jar meat sauce
- Medium diced red onion
- 1 medium diced green pepper
- 6 mashed garlic cloves
- 1 tsp Adobo
- 1 tsp oregano
- 1 packet of Sazon Goya with cilantro y achiote
- 1/2 tsp salt

Recipe:
First on high heat, bring a pot full of water to boil, add salt, and once water starts boiling add your lasagna pasta for 10 minutes, stirring occasionally no more than 2 times. You don't want your pasta to

stick; however, you also don't want it to break apart. Once the pasta is tender, drain the water, and add cold water to the pot to cool.

Next, time to make your saucy ground beef. Season your meat with garlic, oregano, adobo, and Sazon Goya. Mix and set aside. Wash your hands and let's get your pan ready.

Set your pan on your stove on medium-high heat, add your ground beef, and stir occasionally until the meat is browned. You shouldn't see any red on the meat as this will tell you the meat is still raw. Once browned, add onions and peppers. Let it simmer for 2 minutes. Now add meat sauce, simmer again for 2 more minutes, and set aside.

Next, it's time to layer your ingredients. In a lasagna baking pan, your first layer will be 3–4 lasagna pasta depending on the width of your pan, making it nice and tight. Then add your meat, ricotta, and finally a generous amount of cheese. Continue this layering pattern until the ingredients are done, leaving some cheese for the last layer of lasagna pasta. Once all ingredients are done, dip 3–4 more lasagna pasta into the leftover meat sauce from the pan and cover the last layer with it. This will give it a nice color and will keep it nice and moist. Otherwise, it will get crispy once it's exposed to the heat in the oven when broiling. Layer it with the remaining cheese and bake at 350 degrees covered for 20 minutes, then uncover and broil at 400 degrees for 5 minutes. Let cool for 10 minutes, cut into squares, and serve with garlic bread or on its own. Enjoy!

Dary's Dominican Beans

These beans are to die for! As a little girl, my mother would make these almost every day. It reminds me of when dinner was ready, and I would sit at the dining table, swinging my legs back and forth, excitedly waiting to get served. This bean recipe is a staple in a Dominican household. It personally brings me so much warmth and happiness in my soul. Get ready to savor the most delicious Dominican beans with this recipe!

Ingredients: (serves 12)
- 16 oz bag roman beans
- 1 bunch cilantro
- 1 lime
- 2 tbsp tomato paste
- 1/2 small auyama/pumpkin
- 1tsp adobo
- 1 small red onion
- 1/2 large green pepper
- 1/2 large red pepper
- 2 sopita cubes
- 1 packet of Sazon Goya with cilantro y achiote
- 1tsp oregano
- 6 mashed garlic cloves

Recipe:
Start by boiling beans in a large pot full of water. Boil beans until tender for about 1 hour, adding water occasionally as needed every time it dries up. Once beans are tender, leave about 5 cups of water

in a pot. Add adobo, oregano, cilantro, garlic, onions, squeezed lime, peppers, tomato paste, sopita, Sazon Goya, and auyama. Simmer on medium-low heat for 10 minutes. Serve with white rice and your favorite side dish. Enjoy!

Dary's Cheese Steak Sliders

This is my favorite type of slider. I can eat six of these without stopping. I learned how to make these as an adult. I love Philly cheesesteak sandwiches, so I decided to make them into sliders to easily be able to share with my large group of family and friends. Everyone will forever fall in love with these! Perfect for the Super Bowl, family dinner, movie night with the kids, or just a meal you can indulge in on your own.

Ingredients: (serving size 24 sliders)
- 24-pack Hawaiian sliders
- 2 pounds sliced palomilla steak or stir fry steak.
- 1/2 pound Provolone cheese
- 1/2 cup mayonnaise
- 1 medium diced red onion
- 1 medium diced green pepper
- 6 mashed garlic cloves
- 1 tsp oregano
- 1 tsp adobo
- 1 cup vinegar
- 1/2 lime
- 1/2 cup oil

Recipe:
First, clean your meat with vinegar, rinse with cold water, drain water, and season. Add adobo, oregano, garlic, and lime. Mix and set aside. Heat a pan on medium-high heat, add oil, then add your steak. Cook until tender for about 30 minutes, occasionally adding

1 cup of water as needed. Once tender, let it simmer in the pan, add onions and peppers, and let it pan fry for two minutes. Add 1/2 cup of water, letting it simmer uncovered for 2 more minutes. You should see some sauce from the juices of the meat, stir, turn off the stove, and set aside.

Next, with a bread knife, cut your Hawaiian bread in half, spread mayonnaise evenly on both sides, and spread steak evenly across the bottom part of the bread. Layer the provolone cheese evenly on top of the steak, then cover with the top portion of the bread. Put it in the oven at 350 degrees for 10 minutes, then cut into sliders. I like to add a side of ketchup to my plate, then dip my slider into it. Enjoy!

Dary's Potato Salad

I've always loved potato salad even as a child, but there are so many ways of making it. This recipe I am sharing with you is my favorite and most delicious way of making it. I also sometimes substitute carrots with beets, or I may add both! My technique to make it nice and creamy is a game changer. You will never go back!

Ingredients: (serves 10)
- 5 lb bag potatoes cut in half.
- 1 medium bag carrots
- 6 eggs
- 1 large diced red onion.
- 1/2 cup vinegar
- 1 tsp salt

Recipe:
Bring a pot full of water to boil, add salt, then add potatoes, carrots, and eggs. Boil eggs for 10 minutes and remove from water and set aside. Let vegetables boil until tender for an additional 20 minutes. In the meantime, in a small bowl, add your onions, vinegar, and a pinch of salt and let marinade. Once vegetables are tender, drain water and let cool. Once cooled, dice carrots, potatoes, and eggs. Add to a large bowl, add mayonnaise, a pinch of salt, onions, and 1/4 cup of the remaining vinegar. Mix it all together, mashing it with your spoon just a bit about 4 times to give it a creamier texture. Taste. If you like it with more salt, add another pinch of salt. Serve and enjoy!

Dary's Chicken Quesadillas

Those who know me know how obsessed I am with Mexican food. I can eat Mexican food every single day of my life. This chicken quesadilla recipe is the best you'll ever have! Tasty, cheesy, and delicious!

Ingredients: (serving size, 20 quesadillas)
- 10 flour tortillas
- 1lb chicken breast- cut into small cubes.
- 1 large chopped tomato.
- 1 small diced red onion.
- 1 small diced green pepper
- 16 oz shredded cheddar cheese
- 6 mashed garlic cloves
- 1 tsp adobo
- 1 tsp oregano
- 1 packet of Sazon Goya with cilantro y achiote
- 1 tsp sugar
- 1/2 cup butter
- 1/4 cup oil
- 1/2 squeezed lime

Recipe:
First, clean your meat with vinegar and water. Lather, rinse with cold water, and on a cutting board, cut your chicken into small cubes. Season with, garlic, adobo, oregano, lime, and Sazon Goya. Mix and set aside. Heat a pan on medium-high heat. Add oil and then sugar for caramelization. Let sugar brown to a dark caramel color, not black

or the sugar will end up burning making your chicken taste bitter. Once caramelized, add chicken. Stir your chicken so both sides have that beautiful golden-brown color. Let it cook for 10 minutes. You will notice the liquid in the pan drying out, and pan starting to sizzle, now it's the perfect time to add your onions, peppers, and tomatoes. Stir your vegetables while at the same time scrapping the brown parts from the pan. Next, add 1/2 cup of water and simmer for two minutes. It will have a very light sauce and vegetables will be more translucent in color. Set aside.

Finally, you want to add the chicken to half of the flour tortillas and add a generous amount of cheese. The more cheese, the cheesier it will be. Close the tortillas with the other side. Heat a nonstick pan on low heat, add 1 tsp of butter, and add your filled tortillas. Cook tortillas for about a minute until golden brown on both sides. Remove from pan and cut tortillas in half. Serve with a side of sour cream, salsa, guacamole, or by itself! Enjoy!

Dary's Macaroni Tuna Salad

This macaroni tuna salad is to die for! Superrich, flavorful, creamy, and delicious. My mouth is watering as I am writing this. Quick and super easy recipe you can make and enjoy with your family. My kids love it!

Ingredients: (serves 10)
- 6 tuna cans in oil
- 1 cup mayonnaise
- 1 large diced green pepper
- 1 box macaroni pasta
- 1/2 cup Dijon mustard
- 1 tbs olive oil
- 1 tsp adobo
- 1 tsp vinegar
- 1 tsp oregano
- 1 packet of Sazon Goya with cilantro y achiote
- 1 tsp salt
- 1 small diced red onion

Recipe:
First, thing you want to do is fill up a large pot of water, add salt, and let boil. Once boiling starts add pasta, continuously mixing until tender for 10 minutes. You will notice the pasta has doubled in size and has become more translucent in color. Drain water and add pasta to a large bowl where you will be serving it once done. To the bowl, add tuna, including the oil from the can, peppers, onions, adobo, oregano, Sazon Goya, vinegar, olive oil, Dijon mustard, and mayonnaise. Mix thoroughly. Serve with crackers or as a side dish with your dinner. Delicious on its own as well. Enjoy!

Dary's Three-Cheese Ziti Pasta

I love a nice cheesy, saucy pasta, so instead of placing the cheese on top once my pasta is done, I mix in my favorite 3-cheeses into my saucy pasta all together. Growing up, my parents never really switched it up in the kitchen. It was usually rice and beans with some sort of meat, or we would go to Chinatown and buy fresh seafood for dinner and make it with fried plantains or rice and beans. I love switching it up in my kitchen, and when I feel in the mood for a change, this recipe is one of my go-to. This is a quick and delicious recipe everyone will love!

Ingredients: (serves 8)
- 1 box ziti pasta
- 1 large jar meat sauce
- 1 lb 80/20 fat ground beef
- 1/2 and 8 oz bag of shredded mozzarella cheese
- 1/2 an 8 oz bag of cheddar cheese
- 3 tbs grated parmigiana cheese.
- 1 tsp hot sauce (optional)
- 1 small diced red onion.
- 1 small diced green pepper
- 6 mashed garlic cloves
- 1 tsp adobo
- 1 tsp oregano
- 1 packet of Sazon Goya with cilantro y achiote
- 1/2 tsp salt

Recipe:

For this recipe, I start by making my ground beef. I make it the same way I make it for my lasagna recipe. I season it with adobo, oregano, garlic, and Sazon Goya. I added it to my pan on medium-high heat until brown thoroughly. I then add peppers and onion, let it simmer for 2 minutes, then add my meat sauce. Simmer again for 2 more minutes and all done! If I am in the mood for some spice, I add 1 tsp of my favorite chipotle hot sauce, or you can use your favorite. Set aside and now start making your pasta.

Fill up a pot of water and add salt, let boil and add the ziti pasta for 10 minutes, stirring occasionally so it doesn't stick together. Once done, drain and add pasta to your saucy ground beef. Add all 3 cheeses, mix, and cook for 2 minutes as the cheese melts. Serve with fried plantains, garlic bread, or on its own. Enjoy!

Dary's Saucy Meatballs

I honestly had never tried meatballs growing up until I met my husband. One day he invited me over to his mother's house for dinner when we were first dating. I remember my mother-in-law made meatballs with rice and beans and a green salad. I remember being skeptical because I had never tried meatballs and was a very picky eater at that time. I didn't want to be rude, so I tried it, and wow, my mouth burst with flavors, and my love for meatballs had begun. This is also my husband's favorite meal, so I had to perfect it. This recipe is inspired by my mother-in-law with my own twist and favorite ingredients.

Ingredients: (serves 6)
- 1 lb 80/20 ground beef
- 1 egg
- 1/2 cup breadcrumbs
- 6 mashed garlic cloves
- 1 tsp oregano
- 1 tsp adobo
- 1 packet of Sazon Goya with cilantro y achiote
- 1 tbs tomato paste
- 1/2 cup water
- 1 small diced red onion.
- 1 large diced green pepper
- 1 tsp sugar
- 3 tbs oil

Recipe:

   In a bowl, add ground beef, adobo, oregano, garlic, Sazon Goya, breadcrumbs, and egg. Mix, and form your meatballs. I like mine medium-sized like a golf ball. In a separate pan on medium-high heat, add oil and sugar, and let the sugar caramelize until golden brown. Once caramelized, add your meatballs all around your pan and let brown on both sides. Cook for 5 minutes on both sides, then add onions and peppers. Sauté for 2 minutes, add tomato paste and water, stir, and simmer again for 5 more minutes. Serve with rice and beans, moro, fried plantains, side of pasta, or as a meatball sandwich. Enjoy!

Dary's Saucy Shrimp

Ahhhh! Shrimp, shrimp, shrimp! My favorite seafood. This recipe is by far my favorite way of making shrimp. It is juicy, flavorful, hearty, and delicious. So many ways you can pair this or just enjoy on its own. Super quick and easy to make. Another meal everyone will love!

Ingredients:
- 3 lb large peeled and divined shrimp
- 3 limes
- 1 medium diced red onion
- 1 medium diced green pepper
- 1 tsp oregano
- 1 tsp adobo
- 6 mashed garlic cloves
- 1 packet of Sazon Goya with cilantro y achiote
- 3 tbs oil
- 2 tbs tomato paste
- 1 cup water

Recipe:
First, clean your shrimp with 2 limes, rinse with cold water, and drain water. Season with 1 lime, adobo, oregano, garlic, Sazon Goya. Mix and set aside. In a large pot or pan on low heat, add garlic, onions, and pepper. Let it simmer for 2 minutes, now add shrimp, and cook for 2 minutes until shrimp is pink all around. Next, add tomato paste and water. Simmer once more for about a minute and stir. Serve with a side of fried plantains or white rice. Enjoy!

Dary's Fried Chicken

If you are a fried chicken lover, this one is for you! This is my go-to fried chicken recipe. The crispiness and juiciness of this chicken are unmatched. For a twist, I also sometimes add Dijon mustard when seasoning the chicken. Try them both!

Ingredients:
- 1 family pack boneless chicken thighs (8-10 pieces)
- 1 tbs adobo
- 1 tbs oregano
- 6 mashed garlic cloves
- 1 squeezed lime
- 5 cups flour
- 10 cups oil
- 1 cup vinegar

Recipe:
First, clean your chicken with vinegar, lathering as you go. Rinse with cold water and start seasoning. Season with adobo, oregano, garlic, and lime. Mix and set aside. In another bowl, add flour and add 3–4 chicken at a time to the flour, not removing any excess flour. This is what makes it nice and crispy. Next, in a frying pan, add your oil, making sure your pan is filled up with oil halfway. Set on high heat, and once hot, add your chicken, and immediately change the temperature to medium-high heat. Once golden brown, turn to the other side, and once both sides are golden brown, remove from the pan. Transfer over to a plate with a napkin so it can soak up any excess oil. Repeat the temperature change each time you add

a new batch of chicken. This is also what helps with slowly creating that crispy texture on the outside while keeping the inside juicy and delicious. Serve with homemade french fries, fried plantains, or rice and beans. Enjoy!